B-82

Christmas Classics
by Sue Saltkill

- **More than 50 quick, easy to sew projects**
- **Designs feature Scottie dogs, penguins, folk-art Santas**
- **Ornaments • Wreaths • Decorations • Gifts**
- **Written by the author of Country Christmas**

Introduction

Webster defines classic as being correct for a variety of places and occasions, and basically in fashion year after year. "Classic" also refers to a design that has become a standard. The many exciting projects in **Christmas Classics** are good examples, from the traditional Dan River plaids to the classic design themes of Scottie dogs, houses, penguins, snowmen, and hearts.

Let the ideas in this book inspire you to make holiday gifts or to decorate your home with **"Christmas Classics"**.

Acknowledgements

A special thanks to Susan Wilson for making the Braided Heart Rug, Nancy Martin for the Heart Doll Quilt, and Sue Thompson for the Crocheted Placemats.

Table of Contents

General Directions 3
Supplies 3
Kitchen Classics 4
    Kitchen Towels, Crochet Place Mats, Napkins, Napkin Ring, House Potholder, Hostess Apron, Christmas Basket, Folk Doll Appliance Cover
Gifts for Children 9
    Sweatshirts, Baby Bib, Tote Bag, Scottie Stick Puppet, Clown Stick Puppet, Santa Stick Puppet, Yoyo Clown, Sock Monkey, Kris Kringle, Holly Days, Toy Soldier
Scottie's Tree 14
    Scottie's Treats, Scottie's Wreath, Scottie Ornament, Butterfly Ornament, Plaid Fan Ornament, Scottie's Basket, Straw Hat Ornament, Tree Skirt, Christmas Stocking
Scottie 17
    Scottie Pillow, Scottie Quilt, Stuffed Scotties
For the Men 18
    Jean Pillow, House Quilt, Stuffed Duck, Denim Pillow, Chef's Apron, Gardener's Apron, Map Pack, Log Carrier
Let It Snow 23
    Sock Snowman, Yarn Snowman, Stuffed Snowman
Wreaths and Decorations 24
    Decorated Broom, Ruffled Wreath, Button Wreath, Hydrangea Wreath, Cornhusk Wreath, Decorated Grapevine Wreaths
A Hearfelt Christmas 26
    Heart Wreath, Heart Doll Quilt, Braided Heart Rug, Checkerboard Wall Hanging
Glossary of Techniques 29

Christmas Classics©

© Sue Saltkill, 1985

Credits:
Photography . . . . Carl Murray
Graphics . . . . Stephanie Benson
Illustration . . . . Nicki Salvin Wight
Plaid fabrics courtesy of Dan River, Inc.

0-943574-32-3

That Patchwork Place™

General Directions

Read through the list of materials needed before you begin a craft or sewing project. Have all the necessary materials on hand and become familiar with the construction directions before you proceed.

All pattern pieces are printed on the pull-out pattern section, stapled in the center of the book. Open staple to remove pages. Reclose staple to keep book intact. Store pattern pieces in a large manilla envelope glued to inside of back cover.

Pattern pieces are full-size, so it will not be necessary to graph or enlarge patterns. Dimensions, rather than pattern pieces, are given for patterns that are a simple square, rectangle, triangle or circle.

Do not cut pattern pieces from pattern page or you will destroy patterns on the reverse side. Instead, trace patterns onto tissue paper or pattern paper, making sure to include all lines and markings. You may wish to fold pattern paper in half to make a complete pattern piece for those pieces marked "place on fold".

Be certain to mark all lines, dots, and notches onto the traced patterns. All seams are 1/4" and all fabrics are sewn together with right sides of fabric facing unless otherwise indicated.

Examine photographs and illustrations to see what an item looks like when completed.

In many cases, you will need only a scrap of fabric for your projects. You may use any suitable scrap of fabric that you have. Our materials lists indicate that 1/8 yd. of fabric is necessary because that is the least amount of fabric you can buy. You can expect to have fabric left over.

Supplies

Fabric

To achieve the traditional "classic" look in our Christmas items, we used a variety of plaid fabrics from the "Glad Tidings" collection by Dan River. These crisp woven plaids are perfect for our projects and will be available this season at your local fabric shop. For all projects in this book, yardage requirements specify the amount and type of fabric, and in many cases color recommendations. Feel free to adapt the fabric and color to your own decor, adding your own creative variations. Yardage amounts are based on 44"-wide fabric. Preshrink and press fabrics before cutting, except when using corduroy, satin or velvet.

Ribbons and Trims

Trims must be selected carefully to achieve the desired results. Study the photographs and select similar trims. It is important to use ribbons in the widths specified.

Thread

For strength and durability, especially for applique, use a good quality thread, such as cotton-wrapped polyester or cotton. Carefully match thread colors to fabric.

Batting and Stuffing

Mountain Mist® Fiberloft® polyester stuffing is recommended for projects requiring stuffing. It is available wherever fabric is sold. Mountain Mist® quilt batting is recommended for hand quilted items to give projects a nice finished look. Needlepunch batting has been used as both batting and stabilizer in machine sewn items.

Scissors

Use a good, sharp pair of scissors to cut fabric and an older pair for cutting patterns. Use embroidery scissors to cut small applique pieces and ribbons.

Rotary Cutter and Mat

A rotary cutter and mat will save a great deal of time cutting strips for crocheting and bias strips for binding.

Fusible Webbing

Fusible webbing is a bonding agent for fabric. A fairly permanent bond results from applying heat and pressure with an iron. Refer to manufacturer's directions for best results.

When cutting applique motifs, place fusible webbing behind fabric, pin in place, and cut motifs as a single unit. Leave pins in place until you are ready to fuse to background fabric.

Aleene's Tacky Glue™

Aleene's Tacky Glue™ is a clear pliable water based craft glue that does not soak through fabrics.

Glue Stick

A glue stick is a water-based bonding agent in a tube applicator and is recommended for securing applique pieces. It can also be used as an alternative to pins, hand basting or fusible webbing.

Glue Gun

A glue gun is useful for attaching trims. Carefully read the manufacturer's instructions and follow suggested safety procedures.

Water Erasable Marker

The ink in a water erasable marker is easily removed with a damp cloth or cotton swab. The markers are available in needlework and fabric shops. Follow the manufacturer's directions. Always test pen on a scrap of the fabric to be marked. Mark only dark enough for lines to be visible.

Kitchen Classics

Decorate your kitchen for Christmas using Classic Dan River plaids. Crochet placemats from strips of plaid fabric and add co-ordinating potholders, kitchen tools, napkins and napkin rings. Wear your hostess apron while you serve Christmas goodies from a gay Christmas basket lined with plaid fabric.

The classic folk doll appliance cover has been found in kitchens for years. "Mandy" or "Aunt Jemima" was originally made as a toaster cover. By lengthening or shortening the skirt this cover can be adapted to fit can openers, mixers, food processors and other kitchen appliances.

Kitchen Towels

Materials:

Woven dish towel,
    approximately 18" x 28"
Scrap of plaid fabric for
    applique
Fusible webbing

Directions:

1. Cut heart appliques from plaid fabric and fusible webbing. Fuse to dish towel.

2. Machine applique hearts to dish towel following directions given in the Glossary.

Crochet Place Mats

Finished size: approximately 13" x 17"

Materials:

3 yds. plaid fabric per placemat
Size J or –10 crochet hook

Directions:

1. Prewash fabric. Remove selvages. Use rotary cutter or tear into 1" strips across the grain of fabric (from selvage to selvage).

2. Stitch strips together by machine using a 1/4" seam. Roll into a ball.

3. Make a slipknot near end of fabric leaving a 5" tail. Loosely chain.

4. Row 1: Skip first stitch and single crochet back to the end. Now make 2 single crochets in the end stitch. (This "turns" corner and helps placemat to lie flat.)

5. Row 2: Single crochet back to opposite end. Make 2 single crochets in end stitch to "turn" corner. Single crochet back to opposite end.

6. Rows 3-13: Continue in the same manner, making 2 single crochets in the end stitch or as necessary to maintain oval shape and have placemat lie flat*, until placemat is 13" x 17" or desired size.

7. Cut off end leaving a 5" tail. Tie a knot, then weave beginning and ending tails into placemat.

8. Block with a damp pressing cloth and iron to lie flat.

* Crocheting loosely will help to maintain flatness, but you may need to add an extra single crochet at the corners to keep placemat flat.

Napkins

Finished Size: 15 1/2" x 15 1/2"

Materials:

1/2 yd. fabric

Directions:

1. For each napkin, cut a 16" x 16" fabric square. Finish all edges in narrow hem.

Napkin Ring

Materials:

Plaid Fan Ornament
2" diameter plastic ring

Directions:

1. Construct plaid fan ornament using directions given on page 15.

2. Stitch the 2" diameter ring to back of fan ornament along center fold, approximately two inches from lower edge.

House Potholder

Finished size 7" x 7"

Materials:

Two 7 1/2" x 7 1/2" squares
    needlepunch
Two 7 1/2" x 7 1/2" pieces solid
    fabric for potholder front and
    backing
7 1/2" x 7 1/2" plaid fabric
7 1/2" x 7 1/2" fusible webbing

Directions:

1. Using the 7" House Applique pattern, cut house and roof pieces from plaid fabric and fusible webbing. Fuse to solid background fabric.

2. Baste needlpunch to wrong side of potholder front and backing.

3. Machine applique house to background following directions given in the Glossary.

4. Construct a 2" double fold strip from plaid fabric following directions given in the Glossary. Pin raw edges to one corner of the potholder to serve as a loop. Baste in place.

5. Pin potholder front to backing with right sides together.

6. Clip corners, trim the seams, and turn the potholder to the right side.

7. Stitch the opening closed and topstitch 1/4" from finished edges.

Hostess Apron

Finished Size: one size fits all

Materials:
1 3/4 yds. plaid fabric
1/4 yd. green fabric for applique
Fusible webbing

Directions:
1. Cut fabric for hostess apron.

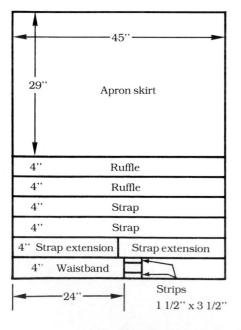

2. With right sides together, fold fabric strips for ruffle in half lengthwise. Run a row of gathering stitches along raw edges, curving stitching at ends of ruffle (see diagram).

3. Gather until each ruffle measures 20" long.

4. With right sides together, seam strap to strap extension along narrow edges.

5. Pin a ruffle to long edge of each strap, beginning 1" from strap end. With ruffle inside, fold strap in half and pin raw edges together, being careful not to catch ruffle. Stitch 1/4" from outside edges of strap, leaving an end open for turning.

6. Turn straps and press.

7. Cut heart from green fabric and fusible webbing. Fuse heart to apron bib. Machine applique following directions given in Glossary. Stitch apron bibs together in a 1/4" seam leaving an opening for turning. Clip corners. Turn. Press. Sew apron bib to ruffled strap, stitching close to end of strap. Backstitch for strength.

8. Hem side and bottom edges of apron skirt by hand or machine.

9. Make two double fold fabric strips, each 3 1/2" long, for waistband ends.

Waistband

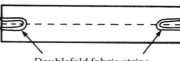

Doublefold fabric strips

10. With right sides together, fold waistband, keeping all raw edges even. Stitch in a 1/4" seam. Turn to right side.

Fold

Stitch

11. Sew a row of gathering stitches across waist edge of apron skirt. Adjust gathers so apron skirt fits waistband. With right sides together, sew one edge of waistband to apron in a 1/4" seam. Press the seam allowance toward the waistband. Press under 1/4" on remaining waistband edge and pin in place on inside of apron.

12. Hand stitch waistband facing in place.

13. Center apron bib on the waistband with bib raw edges behind the waistband. Pin in place. Topstitch 1/4" from all edges to attach apron bib.

14. Apron is worn by crossing straps in back and pulling strap through double fold loop, and tying straps in a bow.

Christmas Basket

Finished size varies

Materials:
Inexpensive chip basket
3/4 yd. plaid fabric*
2 1/2 yds. 1 1/2"-wide pre-
    gathered eyelet
2 1/2 yds. 1"-wide grosgrain
    ribbon
Needlepunch batting
Red craft paint

*fabric amount will vary with
    size of basket

Directions:
1. Measure the basket bottom and cut a rectangle of fabric to fit, adding 1/4" to all edges. Round off the corners. Using the fabric as a pattern, cut a piece of batting the same size. Baste the fabric to the batting.

2. Measure the height of the basket and around outside of rim. For the sides of the basket lining, you will need to cut two rectangles of fabric according to the following measurements: height of basket plus outside rim plus 1/4" seam allowance plus 2 1/4" for drawstring casing equals height; length around the entire basket top plus 1/2" for seams equals length. (Since you are cutting two pieces of fabric, this length will allow enough fabric for shirring.)

Length + 1/2"

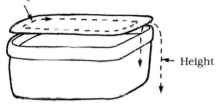

← Height

3. Cut out the lining pieces and stitch, with right sides together, in a 1/4" seam leaving the last 3" of the seam unsewn. This allows the basket lining to slip around the handles.

4. Sew a gathering stitch 1/4" from the lower edge of the basket lining. Pull the thread to adjust the gathers and pin to the basket bottom fabric, with right sides together. Stitch in a 1/4" seam.

5. Press the upper edge of the basket lining 1/4" to the wrong side. Fold again 2" to the wrong side to form the drawstring casing. Stitch close to the folded raw edge. Stitch 1" from the first stitching.

6. Stitch encased edge of pregathered eyelet underneath folded edge of lining.

7. Cut ribbon in half. Using a safety pin, pull the ribbon through the casing on one side of the basket lining. Repeat the process with the remaining ribbon and the other half of the basket lining.

8. Place the lining in the basket, folding the upper edge over the basket rim. Pull the ribbon to gather the fabric and tie in bows at the ends of each basket handle. You may want to tuck in a small piece of fabric below the handle to hide the part of the basket which is not covered by the basket lining.

Folk Doll Appliance Cover

Fits appliances up to 12" tall

Materials:
1/2 yd. brown fabric for body
5/8 yd. fabric for dress
1/4 yd. white fabric for apron
1/8 yd. fabric for bandana
1 1/4 yd. 1 1/2"-wide pre-gathered eyelet trim
2 small buttons for eyes
1/4 yd. 1/4" wide ribbon
Red embroidery floss
1 package red rick rack
5" x 7" piece sturdy cardboard
Mountain Mist® Fiberloft® stuffing

Directions:
1. Cut pattern pieces from fabric. For dress bottom cut a 15" x 45" piece of fabric. For top of dress, cut two strips of fabric 3" x 10".

2. Stitch small button eyes to body front. Embroider mouth using an outline stitch.

3. Stitch body front to body back in a 1/4" seam, leaving lower edge open. Trim corners and clip curves. Turn to right side.

4. Stuff body firmly, ending 2 1/2" from the lower edge. Machine stitch a line 2 1/2" from lower edge to hold stuffing in place.

5. Center lower unstuffed portion on cardboard and staple securely.

6. For dress top, fold each 3" x 10" strip of fabric in half lengthwise. Stitch in a 1/4" seam along long edge. Turn. Press.

7. Stitch rick rack along both long edges.

8. Stitch apron to apron backing in a 1/4" seam along side and lower edges. Trim corners. Turn. Press. Top stitch 1/8" from finished edge.

9. Machine applique tiny heart to apron front following Machine Applique directions in Glossary.

10. Stitch dress bottom along back seam, ending stitching 6" from waistline edge. Press seam open.

11. Narrow hem lower edge of dress bottom. With right sides

together, stitch pre-gathered eyelet to lower edge of dress bottom.

12. On outside of dress, stitch rick rack over lower seam.

13. Center apron along waistline of dress bottom. Baste in place.

14. Gather waistline edge of dress bottom. Draw up gathering thread so that waistline measures 9".

15. Cut a 2" by 20" strip of apron fabric for waistband. With right sides together, stitch one long edge of waistband to gathered dress bottom, leaving 5 1/2" of waistband unstitched on each end.

16. Fold under raw edge of waistband to inside, even with seamline. Stitch 1/8" from folded edges of apron waistband through gathered dress bottom.

17. Baste strips of fabric for dress top to waistband front. Tack strips together at back.

18. Dress is placed over doll's head and tied at back. Back straps are tucked into waistband.

Bandana

1. Cut pattern pieces from fabric. Place right sides together and stitch in a 1/4" seam, leaving an opening along straight edge for turning.

2. Trim corners. Turn to right side and press.

3. Fold bandana as directed on the pattern piece. Stitch along top through all three layers on outside of bandana.

4. Tie ribbon into a small bow and tack to top of bandana.

Ho Ho
Ho

Gifts for Children

Mix and match the Scottie, house, or penguin appliques on sweatshirts, tote bags, and baby bibs for personalized gifts that children will love. Make stick puppets to provide youngsters with hours of fun during the holidays or choose a "Christmas Classic" to make for a special child, such as the sock monkey or yoyo clown.

Sweatshirts

Finished size varies

Materials:
Purchased sweatshirt
Scraps of fabric for applique
Fusible webbing

Directions:
1. Prewash and dry sweatshirt and fabrics.
2. Cut fabric and fusible webbing for 8" Scottie, Penguin, or House applique.
3. Fuse fabrics to sweatshirt in their numbered sequence.
4. Machine applique to sweatshirt following directions given in the Glossary.

Baby Bib

Finished size: 10" x 12"

Materials:
1/3 yd. fabric
Needlepunch
Scraps of fabric for applique
Fusible webbing

Directions:
1. Cut front, lining, and batting from pattern.
2. Cut fabric and fusible webbing for 8" Scottie, Penguin, or House applique.
3. Fuse fabrics to bib in their numbered sequence. Machine applique to bib following directions given in the Glossary.
4. With right sides together and using a 1/4" seam, sew the fabric backing to the front, leaving the top open.
5. Clip curves, turn and press.
6. Top stitch 1/4" around the outside.
7. For ties, turn under both ends of a 30" piece of bias tape. Center on the top of the bib. Pin in place. Stitch.

Tote Bag

Finished size: 14" square

Materials:
3/4 yd. sturdy fabric (canvas, denim, corduroy)
1/4 yd. plaid fabric for trim
1/4 yd. red grosgrain ribbon
Scraps of fabric for applique
Fusible webbing

Directions:
1. Cut the fabric for tote bag, using the diagrammed specifications.

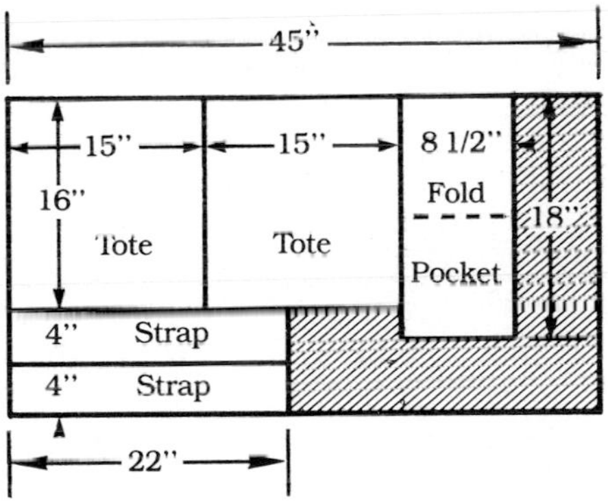

[Diagram: A rectangle labeled 45" wide. Inside it are sections labeled 15", 15", and 8 1/2"; 16" tall on left; "Tote", "Tote", "Fold Pocket"; 18" on right; 4" Strap, 4" Strap; 22" at bottom.]

2. Fold pocket in half, wrong sides together. Press to form top crease, then open flat to applique motif.
3. Cut fabric and fusible webbing for 8" Scottie, Penguin, or House Applique.
4. Fuse fabrics to tote pocket in numbered sequence.
5. Machine applique to pocket following directions given in the Glossary.
6. Fold pocket with right sides together. Stitch 1/4" from remaining three sides, leaving an opening through which to turn. Clip corners.
7. Turn pocket to right side. Stitch opening closed. Press.
8. Cut a 2" square from the bottom of each tote section. The top of this area will mark the bottom of the bag.

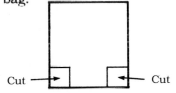

9. Pin pocket to one side of tote. Stitch in place 1/4" from side and lower edges.
10. With right sides facing stitch tote sections together along bottom and side edges using a 1/4" seam. Do not seam 2" square area.
11. Match bottom seam to side seam at lower corner of tote. Sew across this area in a 1/4" seam. Reinforce with another row of stitching. Repeat for remaining lower corner. Now you have formed a box bottom.
12. Cut a 5" x 30" strip of plaid fabric to finish top edge of tote. Fold in half lengthwise and press. Pin raw edges of plaid fabric to inside of tote bag along top edge, overlapping ends of strip. Stitch in a 1/4" seam.
13. Press plaid fabric over tote fabric to form a wide decorative band of fabric. Top stitch lower edge of plaid band to tote, stitching near folded edge.
14. Following directions given in Glossary, make two 2" x 22" plaid double-fold fabric strips to trim tote straps.
15. Fold tote straps with wrong sides together. Press. Encase raw edges of tote straps with plaid double fold strips.
16. Position straps an equal distance from tote sides. Turn under raw ends and pin 2" from top edge on inside of tote. Stitch across straps at top of tote and at folded lower edges.

Santa Stick Puppet

Finished size: 17" high

Materials:

1/4 yd. muslin fabric for head
1/4 yd. fabric for collar and hat
1/8 yd. contrasting fabric for
  collar and hat trim
1 1/4 yds. 1/2"-wide red satin
  ribbon
1/8 yd. 1/8"-wide white ribbon
1/2" diam. wood dowel, 12" long
2 black buttons for eyes
1 red button for nose
Wool roving for beard
Mountain Mist® Fiberloft® stuffing

Directions:

1. Cut pattern pieces and a 5" x 21" strip of fabric for collar.

2. Stitch around head pieces with right sides together in a 1/4" seam. Clip curves. Turn.

3. Stuff head firmly, inserting wood dowel when top of head is fully stuffed. Distribute stuffing evenly around dowel.

4. Gather bottom of head and glue to dowel.

5. Fold the 5" x 21" strip of collar fabric in half lengthwise. Sew a double fold strip of fabric to raw edges as binding. See double fold strips in the Glossary.

6. Run a gathering stitch along folded edge of fabric. Pull thread to gather and glue around raw edges of puppet head.

7. Tie 20" ribbon around neck in a knot. Tie 24" ribbon on top of this into a bow.

8. Cut two hat pieces from fabric. Place wrong sides together and bind curved edge with a double fold fabric strip, following directions given in Glossary.

9. Stitch hat in a 1/4" seam along back. Turn to right side.

10. Stitch a small bell to point of hat. Glue hat to Santa's head.

11. Stitch buttons for eyes and nose in place.

12. Cut a 4" strip of narrow ribbon for beard. Follow directions given on page 12 for making and attaching mustache and beard from wool roving. Roving for mustache will be cut 4" long.

Scottie Stick Puppet

Finished size: 17" high

Materials:

1/4 yd. black fabric
1/8 yd. red dot fabric for applique
1/2 yd. 1/2"-wide red satin ribbon
1/2" diameter wood dowel, 12"
  long
Mountain Mist® Fiberloft® stuffing

Directions:

1. Cut fabric into two   " x   " pieces. Trace Scottie's outline directly onto fabric. Machine applique small red heart onto Scottie.

2. Sew pieces together along the drawn line, leaving an opening through which to turn.

3. Cut off excess fabric 1/4" from stitching line.

4. Clip curves and turn to right side.

5. Stuff Scottie firmly, inserting wood dowel when top of Scottie's body is fully stuffed. Distribute stuffing evenly around dowel.

6. Stitch opening closed around dowel.

7. Tie ribbon into a bow around Scottie's neck.

Clown Stick Puppet

Finished size: 17" high

Materials:

1/4 yd. muslin fabric for head
1/4 yd fabric for collar and hat
1/8 yd. contrasting fabric for
  collar and hat trim
1 1/4 yds. 1/2"-wide red satin
  ribbon
1/2" diameter wood dowel, 12"
  long
2 black buttons for eyes
2 red pompons
Black embroidery floss
Small amount red yarn
Scrap red felt
Mountain Mist® Fiberloft® stuffing

Directions:

1. Cut fabric and assemble, following directions 1-9 of Santa Stick Puppet

2. Thread a large-eye needle with yarn. Make loops of yarn to represent hair, drawing yarn through puppet head.

3. Stitch pompon to point of hat. Glue hat to clown's head.

4. Glue pompon or felt nose in place. Stitch button eyes to head.

5. Embroider mouth outline with black floss on red felt mouth. Glue in place.

Yoyo Clown

Finished size: 18" tall

Materials:

White knit nylon stretch sock
3" diameter styrofoam ball
1/2 yd. **each** red print, white print
  and blue print fabric for yoyos
1/4 yd. fabric for hat and ruff
1/8 yd. fabric for trim
9 1/2" x 12" red felt square
2 small black buttons
Black embroidery floss
Mountain Mist® batting
Button cord or heavy thread
5 red pompons

Directions:

1. From **each** fabric construct 3 large yoyos for clown body and 12 small yoyos for arms and legs. See Glossary for yoyo instructions.
2. Pull sock over styrofoam ball. Secure at top and bottom of ball with button cord.
3. Cut hands and feet from felt. Stitch together in a 1/4" seam. Clip curves. Turn to right side. Stuff firmly. Stitch opening closed.
4. Thread large needle with double strand of button cord. Attach firmly to clown foot, then string through center of nine small yoyos, alternating colors.
5. Using a second needle and piece of button cord, repeat for remaining clown leg, using fabric yoyos in the same color sequence.
6. Maintaining color sequence, draw both needles through center of nine large yoyos to form clown's body. Secure with knot to lower end of styrofoam ball.
7. Construct and attach ruff for clown following steps 5 and 6 of Santa Stick Puppet on page 10.
8. Attach nine small yoyos to clown hands using the same procedure as used for the legs. Knot thread after attaching nine yoyos. Secure between second and third yoyo of clown's body, knotting thread firmly to center cord. Leave enough slack cord so that arms begin at the edge of yoyo body.
9. Finish clown hat and face using directions 8 and 9 of Santa Stick Puppet and directions 3, 4 and 5 of Clown Stick Puppet on preceding page.

Sock Monkey

Finished size: 16" tall

Materials:

1 pair Nelson Red Heel
  Rockford socks
Red knitting yarn
Mountain Mist® Fiberloft® stuffing
2 small black buttons
Black embroidery floss

Directions:

1. Take first sock and stitch seams 1/2" from center on sock starting three inches from the white heel and across the end of top. Cut sock between seams. This leaves an opening in crotch.

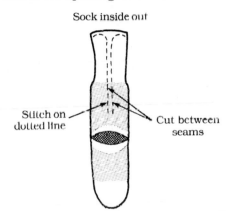

Sock inside out

Stitch on dotted line

Cut between seams

2. Turn sock to right side and use crotch opening to stuff head, body, and legs.
3. Cut the remaining sock into the following pieces:

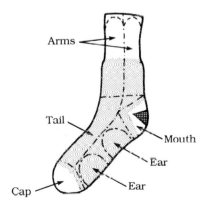

Arms

Tail

Cap

Mouth

Ear

Ear

4. Seam each arm piece together, rounding the ends. Stuff. Attach to body.

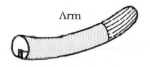

Arm

5. The heel of the sock is used for the mouth. Stuff and fasten to lower part of face with a whip stitch.
6. Stitch ears along curved edges. Turn to right side. Stuff lightly and attach to side of head.

Ears

7. Tail is cut one inch wide. Seam together tapering to a point on the end. Stuff lightly. Attach to body back.

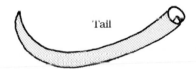

Tail

8. Tie lengths of red yarn at bottom of arms and legs to denote hands and feet.
9. Sew buttons for eyes (or substitute felt or embroidered eyes for very young children). Embroider eyelashes and nose with black embroidery floss.
10. For cap, cut the toe from sock, leaving 1/2" of brown to roll for a brim. Attach a yarn pompon to the top.

*Directions courtesy of The Nelson Knitting Company, Rockford, Illinois.

Important Safety Note

If any of the dolls or puppets are being made for young children, substitute embroidered or felt eyes and nose for button eyes and nose.

Kris Kringle

Materials:

1/3 yd. linen or coarsely woven fabric for body and legs

1/2 yd. red or green wool for coat and hat

1/8 yd. black velveteen for boots and arms

1/3 yd. muslin for pants

1/4 yd. fake fur

14" x 12" piece of burlap for pack

1/3 yd. of 1/4" elastic

1# bag Mountain Mist® Fiberloft® stuffing

Wool roving for beard.*

1 red round button for nose

2 black round buttons for eyes (optional)

Snap

Double-fold bias tape

12" of 1/2-wide belting material

Optional: 12" pet collar

*Roving is a carded unspun wool used in weaving, and is available at craft supply or weaving supply stores. A synthetic product can also be used.

Body:

1. With right sides facing, stitch a boot to the bottom of each leg piece.

2. Press seams down.

3. With right sides facing, stitch leg pieces together, leaving the tops open.

4. Clip curves, turn inside out and stuff.

5. Hand or machine baste the top edge closed.

6. With right sides facing, sew arm pieces together leaving the top edge open. Clip, turn and stuff.

7. Pin arms together so that the seams are facing. Baste closed. This seam line will be the center of the arm.

8. Between dots, pin arms to the right side of the body fabric.

9. With the right sides of the body fabric facing, and arms tucked inside, sew together leaving bottom edge open.

10. Clip seams, turn and stuff.

11. Pin legs in place and machine baste legs to body.

12. Slip stitch the opening closed.

Beard, Mustache, Nose and Eyes:

1. Following pattern markings, attach eyes and nose.

2. Cut a 7" piece of narrow fabric strip, ribbon, or bias tape.

3. Cut the roving or beard material in a 9" x 7" piece.

4. Center the tape onto the roving and stitch in place using a long stitch or a zigzag stitch.

5. Fold the roving in half and attach to the face, tacking at both ends and in the middle.

6. Shape the beard if desired.

7. Use a small amount of roving 7" long to make the mustache. Wrap a thread around the center and attach above the beard.

Pants:

1. Stitch the pants together along the back and front seams. Clip curves and press.

2. Stitch double-fold bias tape to the bottom of the pant leg.

3. Sew together along inside leg.

4. To make elastic casing, turn the folded top edge of pants under 1/2" and stitch. Leave a small opening in the back to thread a 12" piece of elastic. Stitch ends of elastic together.

Coat:

1. Cut fur into four 2 1/2" x 18" strips. Reserve one fur strip for hat.

2. With right sides facing, sew shoulder seams.

3. With right sides together, stitch fur to each sleeve bottom. Clip and discard excess fur. Turn and slip stitch along the back seam to form the cuff.

4. Sew coat side seams.

5. From the coat fabric, make a double folded fabric strip 13" long, following directions given in the Glossary.

6. Stitch double folded strip over raw edge of coat neckline.

7. Fold under the left front edge and stitch a 1/2" seam.

8. With right sides facing, stitch a fur strip to right front edge of the coat. Turn and slip stitch remaining fur edge to underside of coat.

9. In the same manner, stitch a fur strip to bottom edge of coat, overlapping fur at right front edge.

10. Attach the snap.

Hat:

1. Gather between the dots on the hat front to fit the hat back.

2. With right sides facing, position the front onto the back and sew together.

3. With right sides facing, stitch fur to the hat along bottom edge. Turn fur and slip stitch along seam line inside hat.

Belt:

Use 1/2" belting available at fabric stores, a 12" pet collar, or an old narrow belt with a small buckle.

Holly Days

Finished size: 24" tall

Materials:

3/4 yd. red velveteen
1/4 yd. plaid fabric for apron and hatband
1/4 yd. muslin for face
1/4 yd. black velveteen for boots and mittens
1/8 yd. contrast fabric for boots
7/8 yd. 1 1/2"-wide pre-gathered eyelet trim
1/2 yd. 1"-wide flat lace trim
Scraps of pink and black felt
Small amount of black yarn
Red embroidery floss
Mountain Mist® Fiberloft® stuffing
Fusible webbing
6 small black buttons for boots
3 white buttons for apron

Directions:

1. Cut face from muslin and fusible webbing. Fuse to front of doll body using the pattern piece as a guide to placement. Machine applique following directions given in the Glossary. Hand embroider mouth with red embroidery floss.

2. Cut pre-gathered eyelet into three 8" lengths. Stitch to top of face, overlapping eyelet in layers and folding under raw edges at both ends.

3. Cut a 2 1/2" x 10" piece of plaid fabric for hat band. Press under top edge 1/4" and lower edge 1". Place above eyelet rows and stitch along top edge only to secure in place.

4. Stitch mittens with right sides together in a 1/4" seam. Clip curves. Turn to right side. Press.

5. Pin mittens to end of arm pieces, making sure thumbs point in the same direction.

6. Stitch arm pieces together in a 1/4" seam. Clip curves. Turn to right side. Press.

7. Cut boot trim from contrasting fabric and webbing. Fuse to boot fronts. Machine applique in place.

8. Stitch boots with right sides together in a 1/4" seam. Clip curves. Turn to right side. Press.

9. Pin arms and boots to body front. Stitch to body front. Stitch body back in a 1/4" seam, leaving an opening for turning. Clip curves. Turn to right side.

10. Stuff doll body firmly. Stitch opening closed.

11. Cut eyes from black felt and hearts from pink felt. Glue to face.

12. Thread a large-eye needle with black yarn. Make loops of yarn to represent hair, drawing yarn through head.

13. Cut a 2" x 14" strip of plaid fabric. Stitch in a 1/4" seam. Turn to right side. Tie into bow. Tack to hat band. Trim raw ends of fabric at an angle.

14. Stitch 3 buttons to each shoe.

Apron:

1. Cut a 7" x 18" piece of fabric for apron skirt. Hem side and lower edges. Stitch flat lace to lower edge.

2. Gather upper edge of apron. Pull thread so top gathered edge is 6" wide. For waistband encase gathered edge in a 36" long double fold strip, following directions in Glossary.

3. Cut two 4" lengths of pre-gathered eyelet. Stitch together along casing. Tack one end of eyelet to apron behind waistband.

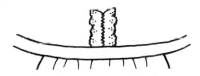

4. Place apron on doll, tying waistband behind back. Fold raw edges of eyelet to inside and tack to body below face. Sew three buttons down the center of eyelet.

Toy Soldier

Finished size: 24" tall

Materials:

3/4 yd. green velveteen
1/8 yd. plaid fabric
1/4 yd. muslin for face
1/4 yd. black velveteen for boots and mittens
1 1/8 yds. 1/2"-wide gold braid trim
Six 3/4" diameter gold buttons
Scraps of black felt
Black pompon
Small amount of black yarn
Red embroidery floss
Fusible webbing
Mountain Mist® Fiberloft® stuffing
Wool roving for mustache

Directions:

1. Stitch gold trim to front of doll using pattern piece as a guide for placement.

2. Construct body following directions 1-13 of Holly Days, omitting pre-gathered eyelet in Step 2, boot trim in Step 7 and pink felt hearts in Step 12.

3. Use a small amount of wool roving 6" long to make the mustache. Wrap a thread around the center and attach above mouth.

4. Sew pompon to top of hat.

5. Sew six buttons to front.

Mountain Mist® Fiberloft® stuffing
5 small dog biscuits
Glue gun and glue sticks
Floral wire

Directions:

1. Cut black fabric into two 6" x 7" pieces. Trace Scottie's outline directly onto fabric.

2. Sew pieces together, stitching directly on the drawn line and leaving an opening through which to turn.

3. Cut off excess fabric 1/4" from stitching line. Clip corners.

4. Turn. Stuff, and stitch opening closed.

5. Tie red satin ribbon around Scottie's neck into a bow.

6. Weave 1 1/2"-wide ribbon around wreath, tying ends together. Use 2 yards of the 1 1/2"-wide ribbon to make a bow following directions given in the Glossary.

7. Attach bow to wreath with floral wire, covering knot from woven ribbon.

8. Position wreath so bow is at side of wreath. Pierce back of Scottie with a piece of floral wire and wind around wreath to attach Scottie.

9. Glue dog biscuits to wreath.

Scottie Ornament

Finished size: 4" x 6"

Materials:

1/4 yd. pre-quilted plaid fabric
3/8 yd. 1/4"-wide red satin ribbon
Mountain Mist® Fiberloft® stuffing

Directions:

1. Cut fabric into two 7 1/2" x 7 1/2" bias pieces. Trace Scottie's outline directly onto wrong side of fabric.

2. Sew pieces together, stitching directly on the drawn line and leaving an opening for turning.

3. Cut off excess fabric 1/4" from stitching line. Clip corners.

4. Turn, stuff, and stitch opening closed.

5. Tie red satin ribbon around Scottie's neck into a bow.

6. Pierce stitching with wire ornament hanger and use to hang.

Scottie's Tree

Scottie's Christmas tree is a very special tree decorated with Scottie ornaments and baskets full of bones for Scottie. Red balls decorated with coordinating plaid ribbon complete the decorations.

Scottie's Treats

Finished size: 2" tall

Materials:

Medium size dog biscuits
1/4 yd. 3/8"-wide red satin ribbon

Directions:

1. Tie ribbon around center of dog biscuit in a knot.

2. Tie a second knot near ribbon ends. Use this loop to hang dog biscuits on tree.

Scottie Wreath

Finished size: 14" diameter

Materials:

14" grapevine wreath
3 yds. 1 1/2"-wide fabric ribbon Scottie print)
1/4 yd. black fabric
3/8 yd. 1/4"-wide red satin ribbon

Butterfly Ornament

Finished size: 5" tall

Materials:

1/4 yd. plaid fabric
3/4 yd. 1/2"-wide flat lace trim
Wooden clothespin
Green craft paint
Gold pipe cleaner
Fray Check™
Aleene's Tacky Glue™

Directions:

1. Cut clothespin so that opening is 2 1/2" long.

2. Paint clothespin green

3. Cut fabric 5 1/4" x 6". Apply Fray Check™ to all raw edges following manufacturer's directions.

4. Stitch 1/2"-wide lace to raw edges.

5. Run a row of gathering stitches two inches from the lower edge. Draw up thread to gather tightly.

6. Slip clothespin opening over the center of fabric, easing in fabric fullness.

7. Cut a 2" length of pipe cleaner. Fold in half and glue to head for butterfly antennae.

Plaid Fan Ornament

Finished size: 4" x 8"

Materials:

4" x 12" plaid fabric
4" x 12" piece heavy iron-on interfacing
12" 3/4"-wide scalloped-edge lace
12" 2"-wide lace
18" 3/8"-wide ribbon
Aleene's Tacky Glue™

Directions:

1. Fuse interfacing to the wrong side of fabric.

2. Glue scalloped-edge lace to the top edge of the right side of fabric.

3. Glue 2"-wide lace 1" from the top edge.

4. After the glue has dried, fold embellished fabric into 3/4"-wide accordian pleats.

5. Glue pleats together 1/2" from the bottom. Attach ribbon bow.

6. Hang using wire ornament hook.

Scottie's Basket

Finished size: 2 1/4" tall

Materials:

Red chip basket 2 1/4" tall
Small dog biscuits

Directions:

1. Fill small red chip baskets with dog biscuits. Hang using wire ornament hook.

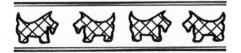

Straw Hat Ornament

Finished size: 3 1/2" diameter

Materials:

Straw doll hat, 3 1/2" diameter
1 yd. 3/8"-wide green ribbon
Red craft paint
Aleene's Tacky Glue™

Directions:

1. Paint hat red.

2. Cut 3/8"-wide ribbon in half. Wrap one piece of ribbon around crown of hat and glue in place with ribbon ends extending downward.

3. Tie second piece of ribbon into a bow. Glue bow on first ribbon, with ends also extending downward.

4. Hang using wire ornament hook.

Christmas Stocking

Finished size: 7" x 18"

Materials:
1/2 yd. pre-quilted plaid fabric
1/4 yd. solid fabric for cuff and facing
1/8 yd. red dot fabric for applique
Mountain Mist® Fiberloft® batting
Fusible webbing
Red embroidery floss

Directions:
1. Cut stocking from pre-quilted plaid fabric. Using an outline stitch and red embroidery floss, embroider line to represent heel.

2. Cut two stocking cuffs and a 4" x 14 1/2" piece of fabric for facing from solid fabric.

3. Cut heart appliques from red dot fabric and fusible webbing.

4. Fuse hearts to stocking cuff. Machine applique following directions given in the Glossary.

5. Cut one stocking cuff from batting. Baste batting behind one stocking cuff.

6. Place two cuff pieces right sides together and stitch in a 1/4" seam. Clip curves and turn to right side. Topstitch 1/4" from curved edges. Baste raw edges together.

7. With right sides together, stitch stocking front to back in a 1/4" seam. Clip curves. Turn.

8. Pin cuff to stocking at upper front edge, making sure applique is visible. Cuff does not extend to back of stocking.

9. Stitch two short ends of facing piece in a 1/4" seam forming a tube. Pin to stocking top, right sides facing.

10. Stitch through all thicknesses in a 1/4" seam.

11. Turn facing to inside and press. Turn under raw edges on lower edge of facing and stitch in place.

12. Make a 7" wide double fold fabric strip following directions in Glossary.

13. Tack raw ends to inside of stocking, forming a loop for hanging.

Tree Skirt

Finished size: 40" diameter

Use scraps of lace to trim this fast and easy eight-section tree skirt. It is an excellent way to show off special plaid fabric and pretty trims.

Materials:
1 3/4 yd. needlepunch batting
1 yd. plaid fabric for panels
1 1/2 yds. fabric for lining
1/4 yd. **each** of five contrasting fabrics: corduroy, velvet and velveteens in shades of red and green.
5 yds. **total** of assorted laces and trims for contrasting panels
4 1/4 yds. 1"-wide flat lace trim

Directions:
1. Cut four tree skirt sections from needlepunch batting.

2. Cut four of each contrasting fabric using tree skirt pattern pieces 1-5. The contrasting fabric should appear in the same position on each panel.

3. Cover needlepunch batting with contrasting fabric, abutting raw edges. Stitch over raw edges with a zigzag stitch.

4. Stitch trims on top of zigzag stitching. Mix and match trims used for panels. It is not necessary to use each trim in the same position on each panel.

5. Complete four tree skirt sections in the same manner. Press.

6. Cut four panels from plaid fabric. Baste needlepunch batting behind each plaid panel. Stitch the plaid and contrasting panels together in a 1/4" seam, right sides together. Alternate plaid and contrasting panels.

7. Cut eight sections of lining; seam together in the same manner.

8. With right sides together, position lining on tree skirt. Stitch in a 1/4" seam, leaving an opening for turning.

9. Clip all inner corners and trim away excess fabric at outer corners. Clip curve. Turn to right side. Press.

10. Hand stitch opening closed. Topstitch 1/4" from outside edges.

11. Stitch lace trim to edge of tree skirt. Ease in extra fullness at the outer corners.

Scottie

Scottie is a real classic among needlework patterns. This charming motif became popular during the term of Franklin Roosevelt with his beloved "Fala". This motif is used as a stuffed animal and to decorate pillows, quilts and wreaths.

Scottie Pillow

Finished size: 18 1/2" x 18 1/2" including ruffle

Materials:

7/8 yd. solid fabric for
   background & ruffle
3/8 yd. plaid fabric for applique
1/4 yd. fusible webbing
1 3/8 yd. 1"-wide pre-gathered
   lace trim
1/4 yd. 3/8"-wide grosgrain ribbon
Small button for eye
Mountain Mist® Fiberloft® stuffing

Directions:

1. Cut Scottie from plaid fabric and fusible webbing. Cut two 12" x 12" squares of solid fabric for pillow front and back and two 8" x 44" strips of fabric for ruffle.

2. Fuse Scottie to pillow front. Cut grosgrain ribbon in half. Pin ribbon ends to Scottie using pattern piece as a guide for placement. Tie ribbon into a bow.

3. Machine applique Scottie to pillow front following directions given in the Glossary.

4. Stitch the two 8" x 44" strips together to form an 8" x 88" strip for ruffle.

5. Follow directions given in Glossary to add ruffle and pre-gathered lace, and to finish pillow.

Scottie Quilt

Finished size: 45" x 45"

Materials:

1 1/8 yd. muslin for background
   fabric
5/8 yd. black fabric for Scotties
5/8 yd. solid fabric for lattice
   strips
3/4 yd. plaid fabric for lattice
   squares and bias binding
1 1/4 yd. fabric for backing
3/4 yd. 1/4"-wide red ribbon for
   collar
Mountain Mist® Fiberloft® stuffing
Fusible webbing

Directions:

1. Cut nine 12" x 12" squares from the background fabric.

2. Cut nine Scottie dogs from black fabric and fusible webbing. Fuse a Scottie dog to the center of each piece of background fabric.

3. Cut nine pieces of grosgrain ribbon each 3" long. Pin in place on Scottie's neck.

4. Machine applique Scottie to background fabric following directions given in the Glossary.

5. Cut 24 lattice strips, each 3" x 12", from solid fabric. Cut 16 lattice squares, each 3" x 3", from plaid fabric.
Note: Bias squares must be staystitched 1/4" from all raw edges to help prevent stretching. You may prefer to place these squares on the grain of fabric.

6. Using 1/4" seams, sew together three lattice strips and four lattice squares. Repeat to make three more units of lattice strips and squares.

7. Using 1/4" seams, sew together four lattice strips and three appliqued blocks. Press all seams away from applique block toward lattice strips. Repeat to make two more rows of lattice strips and applique blocks.

8. Using 1/4" seams, stitch together rows of lattice strips and squares and rows of lattice strips and applique blocks using the Piecing Diagram as a guide. Press all seams away from applique blocks.

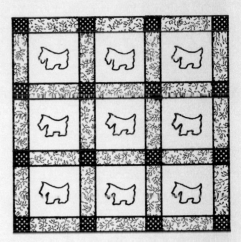

9. Follow the directions given in the Glossary for Preparing to Quilt and Quilting. Scottie Quilt has 1 1/4" diagonal lines quilted through each block. The remainder of the quilting stitches are "in the ditch".

10. Finish quilt with bias binding cut from plaid fabric, following the directions given in the Glossary.

Stuffed Scotties

Finished size: Small, 8 1/2" tall
              Large, 11 1/2" tall

Materials:

1/2 yd. pre-quilted plaid fabric for
   small Scottie
5/8 yd. pre-quilted plaid fabric for
   large Scottie
3/4 yd. 1"-wide satin or grosgrain
   ribbon
Mountain Mist® Fiberloft® stuffing

Directions:

1. Cut from pattern pieces.

2. With right sides together, stitch in a 1/4" seam, leaving an opening for turning.

3. Trim corners and clip curves.

4. Turn, stuff, and stitch opening closed.

5. Tie ribbon around Scottie's neck and into a bow.

For the Men

It has always been difficult to find gift items to sew for men, but here is a collection of both attractive and useful projects. The denim fabrics and crisp plaids combine to make very masculine items.

Jean Pillow

Finished size: 12'' x 12''

Materials:

3/8 yd. pre-quilted plaid fabric
7 1/2'' x 9 1/2'' piece of jeans fabric
3/8 yd. plaid fabric
Mountain Mist® Fiberloft® stuffing

Directions:

1. Cut pre-quilted plaid fabric into two 12 1/2'' x 12 1/2'' pieces.

2. Press side and lower edges of jeans fabric to inside.

3. Center jeans fabric on pre-quilted fabric and stitch close to pressed edges.

4. Cut a 12 1/2'' x 12 1/2'' square of plaid fabric. Narrow hem edges.

5. Fold into quarters and tuck into jeans pocket.

6. Follow directions given in Glossary to finish pillow.

18

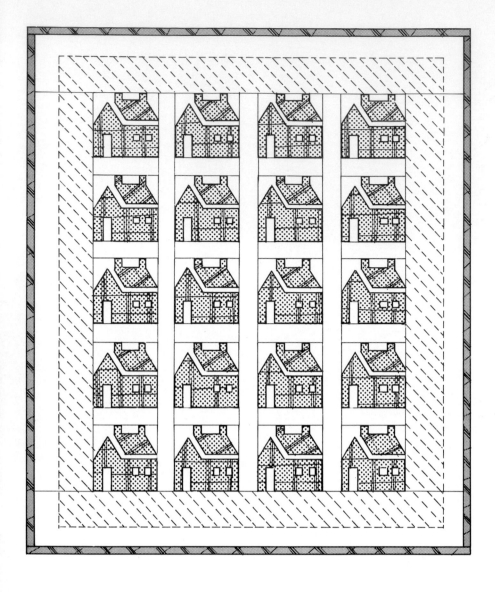

House Quilt

Finished size: 70 1/2" x 84 1/2"

Materials:

5 1/4 yds. plaid fabric for houses, borders and binding
6 yds. dark green fabric for background and lattice
6 yds. fabric for backing
81" x 96" Mountain Mist® batting

Directions:

1. This quilt has simple borders with straight sewn corners. From dark green, cut two 9" x 67 1/2" strips for length and two 9" x 70 1/2" for width.

2. Cut 16 lattice strips 3 1/2" x 11" and three lattice strips 3 1/2" x 67 1/2" from dark green.

3. Using the 11" House Applique pattern, cut house and roof pieces from plaid fabric and fusible web-bing. Cut 20 background blocks 11 1/2" x 11 1/2" from dark green fabric. Fuse houses to solid background fabric.

4. Applique house blocks following Machine Applique directions in Glossary.

5. Set five House blocks together with short lattice strips to make columns. Join four columns of blocks and lattice strips together for quilt top.

6. Add straight sewn borders.

7. Follow the directions given in the Glossary for Preparing to Quilt and Quilting. House Quilt is quilted 1/4" away from houses. The remainder of the quilting is "in the ditch."

8. Finish quilt with bias binding cut from plaid fabric, following the directions in the Glossary.

Stuffed Duck:

Finished size: 12"tall

Materials:

1/2 yd. pre-quilted fabric
3/4 yd. 1"-wide ribbon
Mountain Mist® Fiberloft® stuffing

Directions:

1. Cut fabric from pattern pieces.

2. With right sides together, stitch in a 1/4" seam, leaving an opening for turning.

3. Clip curves. Turn, stuff, and stitch opening closed.

4. Tie ribbon around duck's neck and into a bow.

Denim Pillow

Finished size: 12" x 12"

Materials:

3/8 yd. denim
1/4 yd. plaid fabric for applique and cording
1/4 yd. 3/8"-wide red grosgrain ribbon
Black embroidery floss
Mountain Mist® Fiberloft® stuffing
Fusible webbing

Directions:

1. Cut duck or goose from plaid fabric and fusible webbing. Cut two 12 1/2" x 12 1/2" squares of fabric for pillow front and back from denim.

2. Fuse duck or goose to pillow front. Cut grosgrain ribbon in half. Pin ribbon ends to duck's neck. Tie ribbon into a bow.

3. Machine applique duck or goose to pillow front following directions given in the Glossary.

4. Cut bias binding following directions given in the Glossary.

5. Stitch bias over heavyweight cording.

6. Pin cording to pillow having raw edges even, overlapping ends. Stitch.

7. Follow directions given in Glossary to finish pillow.

Chef's Apron

One size fits all

Materials:

1 yd. fabric for apron and ties
Scraps of fabric for applique
Fusible webbing

Directions:

1. Cut fabric and fusible webbing for 11" Scottie, Penguin, or House applique. Cut apron fabric.

2. Fuse fabrics to apron in their numbered sequence.

3. Machine applique to apron following directions given in the Glossary.

4   Narrow hem top edge of apron. Fold and stitch a narrow hem along apron sides. Do not hem curved edges of apron top.

5. Fold and press curved edges of apron top to inside, forming a 3/4"-wide casing. Stitch close to folded edge of casing, backstitching at each end of seam.

6. Cut two 1 1/2" x 45" strips of fabric for apron drawstring. Stitch together in a 1/4" seam to make a continuous strip. Double fold, press, and stitch as shown in Glossary.

7. Thread each end of drawstring through casing creating a strap to go around neck. To wear apron, adjust drawstrings to form neck opening, cross drawstrings at back, and tie at front of apron.

Gardener's Apron

One size fits all

Materials:

1 yd. fabric for apron, pockets
1/4 yd. plaid fabric for ties
Assorted gardening tools and
   supplies

Directions:

1. Cut fabric from pattern piece using cutting lines marked for Gardener's Apron.

2. Cut an 8" x 42" wide piece of fabric for pockets.

3. Cut a 2" x 42" strip of plaid fabric. Bind upper edge of pocket strip with this fabric.

4. Pin long bound strip of fabric to lower edge of apron with *right side of strip facing wrong side of apron.* Stitch in a 1/4" seam.

5. Turn so pocket is against apron front and press. Stitch lines from top of pocket strip to lower edge varying widths of pockets you are creating. Use the illustration as a guide. Seed packets and peat pots need wider pockets while the handles of gardening tools require narrow pockets.

6. Trim pocket strip to correspond with side edge of apron. Baste. Cut another 2" x 42" strip of plaid fabric. Use to bind apron sides, stitching through both apron and pocket layers.

7. Narrow hem top edge of apron. Do not hem curved edges of apron.

8. Complete apron following Steps 5-7 of Chef's apron.

9. Fill pockets with gardening supplies.

Log Carrier

Materials:

3/4 yd. heavyweight canvas
1/2 yd. plaid fabric
1 package 5/8"-wide doublefold bias tape
Two 3/4" diameter dowels, each 24" long

Directions:

1. Cut canvas 24" x 45".

2. Fold a 4" flap on each end. Cut a semi-circle 6" high by 3" wide in the center of each flap.

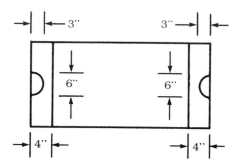

3. Bind with doublefold bias tape.

4. Cut two strips of plaid fabric 8" x 45". Fold in half lengthwise. Press.

5. Pin folded strip to wrong side of carrier placing raw edges of strip 1 3/4" from edge of canvas. Stitch 1/4" from raw edges of strip.

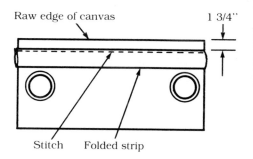

6. Press folded strip to cover seam. Press remainder of strip over canvas edge so that it forms a binding on both the inside and outside of log carrier. Top stitch through all layers close to folded edge of plaid strip.

7. Repeat for remaining side.

8. Bind ends of log carrier with bias tape, folded excess to inside.

9. Fold bound ends of log carrier to inside forming a 4" flap. Stitch in place.

10. Insert dowels into flap at each end to serve as handles.

Map Pack

Finished size: 5 1/4" x 10 1/2" closed, 35" x 10 1/2" open

Materials:

3/8 yd. denim fabric
5/8 yd. plaid fabric

Directions:

1. Cut a rectangle of fabric 11" x 35 1/2" from both denim and plaid fabric. Cut an additional rectangle 10" x 35" from plaid for map pockets.

2. Fold 10" x 35" rectangle in half lengthwise. Baste to right side of large plaid rectangle, having raw edges even.

3. Make a 44" long doublefold strip from plaid, following directions given in the Glossary. Pin at center of short side of map pack.

4. Place right sides together and stitch in a 1/4" seam.

5. Clip corners. Turn to right side. Press.

6. Top stitch 1/4" from all finished edges.

7. For map pockets, top stitch from top of flap to finished lower edge every five inches, creating seven pockets for maps.

8. Fill pockets with area maps, roll to close, and tie with doublefold bias strip.

Let it Snow

Snowmen have become a "classic" holiday pattern ever since we were introduced to "Frosty the Snowman" in 1950. "A corncob pipe and a button nose with two eyes made out of coal" have become design standards. These snowmen, both large and small, are sure to enhance your holiday decor.

(Pictured on back cover)

Sock Snowman

Finished size: 4" tall

Materials:
White ribbed cuff
Small baby sock with stripe trim
Small scrap green felt
Red embroidery floss
Black embroidery floss
Mountain Mist® Fiberloft® stuffing

Directions:
1. Turn sock inside out. Trim away any excess threads.
2. Stuff small amount of fiberfil in toe of sock, forming a round ball, approximately 2 1/2" high.
3. Tie a thread tightly around sock to form snowman's body.
4. Add more stuffing forming a round ball for head. Tie a thread tightly around sock head at top back of sock. Head should be about 1 1/2" high.
5. Fold ribbed cuff of sock down and around head to form a cap.
6. Make a red French knot for nose and embroider mouth using the outline stitch.
7. Add a loop of floss to top of hat for hanging.

1. Frosty the Snowman©, Steve Nelson, Jack Rollins, 1950.

Yarn Snowman

Finished size: 4" tall

Materials:
2 oz. skein 2 ply yarn
Scraps of black felt
Scrap of red felt
1/8 yd. 1/4"-wide red ribbon
Black embroidery floss
Small black felt or plastic hat
Hole punch
Cardboard
Aleene's Tacky Glue™

Directions:
1. Cut a 4" x 5" rectangle of cardboard.
2. For body, wrap yarn around 5" length of cardboard 50 times. Slip small piece of yarn under wrapped yarn, and tie into a tight knot. Cut yarn at exactly the opposite end from tied knot.
3. Tightly tie a small piece of yarn around the body yarn, approximately 1 1/2" from tied knot, to form the head.
4. Wrap yarn around the 4" length of cardboard 50 times for arms. Cut at both ends. Tightly tie a small piece of yarn 1/2" from each end to form hands.
5. Divide yarn for body in half and center yarn arms in between halves. Tie a small piece of yarn 2" from lower ends. This will form "waist" and secure arms in place.
6. Divide remaining yarn in half, forming two legs. Tightly tie a small knot 1/2" from each end to form legs.
7. Using the hole punch, make four black dots and one red dot from felt. Glue in place to represent the eyes, nose, and buttons.
8. Glue small piece of embroidery floss on face to represent mouth.
9. Tie ribbon around neck.
10. Glue small hat to top of head.
11. Tie yarn to back of ribbon, forming a loop for hanging.

Stuffed Snowman

Finished size: 15" tall

Materials:
1/2 yd. sturdy white fabric
1 yd. 1 1/2"-wide plaid ribbon
1 square black felt
Scrap orange felt
5 black pompons
Holly sprig
Small broom
Mountain Mist® Fiberloft® stuffing
Aleene's Tacky Glue™

Directions:
1. Cut Snowman's body using pattern piece. With right sides together, stitch body front to body back in a 1/4" seam, leaving an opening for turning.
2. Clip curves. Turn.
3. Stuff arms. Stitch across arms after stuffing as indicated on pattern piece. Stuff remainder of snowman's body. Stitch opening closed.
4. Cut a 23" length of ribbon. Fringe ends. Tie around snowman's neck.
5. Stitch orange felt for nose. Stuff. Glue to face.
6. Glue black pompons to snowman's body.
7. Tack ends of snowman's arms together. Tack small broom to arms.
8. Tuck holly sprig into ribbon.
9. Cut hat pieces from black felt. Cut a 3 3/4" x 12" piece of black felt for crown of hat. Stitch crown together across short ends. Stitch crown to top of hat. Cut cardboard pieces, omitting 1/4" seam allowance, to stabilize hat. Glue to top and crown on inside of hat.
10. Stitch brim to hat. Glue plaid ribbon for hatband around crown of hat.

Wreaths & Decorations

Brooms and wreaths from dried materials make wonderful holiday decorations both indoors and out. Wreaths also make welcome gifts at Christmas and many can be used year round, such as the hydrangea wreath for a gardener or the button wreath for someone who sews.

Decorated Broom

Finished Size: Varies

Materials:
Purchased broom
6 yds. 2"-wide plaid fabric ribbon
Glass headed pins
Floral wire
Glue gun or thick craft glue
Sprigs of plastic evergreens
Baby's-breath
Decorative plastic cherries

Directions:
1. Begin at the back top of handle and tack ribbon in place; lace ribbon criss-cross down handle. Ribbon should be taut and all tacking, either with pins or glue, should be done on the back side of the broom handle. Two or three yards of ribbon will decorate a handle.

2. With remaining ribbon, make a large loopy bow following directions given in the Glossary.

3. Glue plastic evergreens, baby's-breath and decorative cherries at an angle at base of broom handle.

4. Add bow. Tuck in several loops of decorative ribbon between evergreens.

Ruffled Wreath

Finished size: 18" diameter

Materials:
12" diameter round foam wreath
1 yd. plaid fabric
1/4 yd. fabric for bow
Aleene's Tacky Glue™

Directions:
1. A 12" x 135" piece of fabric is required; cut three 12" strips across the grain of 45"-wide fabric and piece together along the 12" edges to achieve the necessary length. Be sure to cut strips so that plaid will match.

2. Seam together the two long edges in a 1/4" seam, forming a long tube. Turn the tube to the right side. Press so seam is at outside edge. Stitch gathered lace behind outside edge.

3. Measure distance around wreath (see diagram). Divide this dimension in half, then add 1/4". This is the distance you will stitch from the fold to form a casing.

4. Make a cut through the foam wreath.

5. Carefully thread fabric tube onto foam wreath, shirring fabric and distributing gathers evenly around wreath.

6. Glue ends of foam wreath together. To strengthen and stabilize wreath, insert a toothpick to hold sides of wreath together.

7. Adjust gathers again, making sure raw edges of fabric tube are not exposed. Slipstitch raw edges together if desired.

8. Make a fabric bow by cutting a 9" x 45" piece of fabric, slanting ends. Fold in half lengthwise and stitch raw edges in a 1/4" seam, leaving an opening through which to turn. Turn to right side. Stitch opening closed. Press. Tie into a bow and glue to top of wreath.

9. Glue ornament or decoration on top of bow.

Button Wreath

Finished size: 18" diameter

Materials:
12" diameter round foam wreath
1 yd. 45"-wide muslin
3 3/4 yds. 1/2"-wide gathered lace
2 yds. 1 1/2"-wide green ribbon for bow
1/4 yd. 1/4"-wide ribbon for hanging loop
Assortment of green buttons
Aleene's Tacky Glue™

Directions:
1. A 12" x 135" piece of muslin is required; cut three 12" strips across the grain of 45"-wide muslin and piece together along the 12" edges to achieve the necessary length.

2. Seam together the two long edges in a 1/4" seam, forming a long tube. Turn the tube to the right side. Press so seam is at outside edge. Stitch gathered lace behind outside edge.

3. Measure distance around wreath (see diagram). Divide this dimension in half, then add 1/4". This is the distance you will stitch from the fold to form a casing.

4. Make a cut through the foam wreath.

5. Carefully thread fabric tube onto foam wreath, shirring fabric and distributing gathers evenly around wreath.

6. Glue ends of foam wreath together. To strengthen and stabilize wreath, insert a toothpick from one side of splice to the other.

7. Adjust gathers again, making sure raw edges of fabric tube are not exposed. Slipstitch raw edges together if desired.

8. Glue buttons to wreath.

9. Add a large loopy bow with streamers to bottom of wreath.

10. Attach ribbon loop for hanging.

Hydrangea Wreath

Finished size: 20" diameter

Materials:
16" wreath from natural materials
  (grapevine or straw)
2 yds. of 1 1/2"-wide ribbon
Floral wire
Glue gun
Dried hydrangeas*
Baby's breath

Directions:
1. A grapevine wreath works best for this project as hydrangea stems can be tucked in between vines. The natural color of the vines blends with the hydrangeas and helps conceal "open" spaces.

2. Apply glue to hydrangea stems with glue gun and cover grapevine wreath, tucking stems in between vines. Begin at one side of the wreath, gluing hydrangeas in clumps, and work around wreath.

3. Continue using glue gun to apply adhesive to stems of baby's breath and fill in wreath between hydrangeas.

4. Make decorative bow following directions given in the Glossary.

5. Glue bow to top of wreath.

*Note: To cut dry hydrangeas for wreath, select fresh flowers that have not been on plant too long. These blooms will dry to a pink or wine color. Older blooms will turn brown when dried. Tie flowers upside down and dry in a cool dark space.

Cornhusk Wreath

Finished size: 16" diameter

Materials:
16" cornhusk wreath
3 yds. of 1"-wide green
  satin ribbon
Floral wire
Glue gun and hot glue sticks
Decorative plastic cherries

Directions:
1. Wrap ribbon around wreath in a spiral and tie ends together at back of wreath.

2. Make decorative bow following directions given in the Glossary.

3. Attach bow to wreath with glue at lower left curve.

4. Glue decorative plastic cherries in center of bow.

Decorated Grapevine Wreaths

Finished size 16" diameter

Materials:
16" grapevine wreath
3 yds of 1 1/2"-wide ribbon
  (plaid or solid)
Floral wire
Glue gun and hot glue sticks
Ornament or decoration

Directions:
1. Wrap ribbon around wreath in a spiral and tie ends together at back of wreath.

2. Make decorative bow following directions given in the Glossary.

3. Attach bow to top of wreath with glue.

4. Glue ornament or decoration (fresh holly sprigs add a festive touch) at bottom of wreath.

A Heartfelt Christmas

Christmas is a time of loving, giving, and sharing sentiments from the heart. Thus the heart is a perfect symbol to use on decorations, ornaments, gifts, and wrapping paper.

Heart Wreath

Finished size: 10" high

Materials:

10" grapevine heart wreath
1/4 yd. pre-quilted plaid fabric
1 3/4 yds. 3/8"-wide red grosgrain ribbon
Mountain Mist® Fiberloft® stuffing
Floral wire

Directions:

1. Cut fabric into two 6" x 7" bias pieces. Trace outline of duck directly onto fabric.

2. Sew pieces together, stitching directly on the drawn line and leaving an opening through which to turn.

3. Cut off excess fabric 1/4" from stitching line. Clip corners.

4. Turn, stuff, and stitch opening closed.

5. Cut a 12" length of ribbon. Tie around duck's neck.

6. Weave remainder of ribbon around heart wreath. Tie ends in back.

7. Tack duck to ribbon at lower portion of heart. Secure at upper point by piercing fabric with a piece of floral wire attached to wreath.

Heart Doll Quilt

Finished Size: 20" x 24"

Materials:

1/2 yd. light background fabric
1/8 yd. each of five different red prints
1/8 yd. red print for first border
1/8 yd. red print for second border
1/2 yd. red print for outer border and bias binding
5/8 yd. fabric for backing
Mountain Mist® batting

Directions:

1. Cut background fabric 14" x 18". Fold crosswise into fourths. Press creases. Fold lengthwise into fifths. Press creases. This will give you a grid to serve as a guide for the placement of the hearts. Each heart is appliqued in the center of the grid area.

2. Following Paper Patch Applique directions given in the Glossary to make paper templates for 20 hearts. Four hearts will be cut from each red fabric.

3. Applique hearts to background fabric.

4. Cut strips for mitered borders: two strips 1 1/2" x 20" and two strips 1 1/2" x 24" for first border; two strips 1" x 20" and two strips 1" x 24" for second border and two strips 2" x 20" and two strips 2" x 24" for third border.

5. Sew the three strips that comprise each side border, according to diagram. You will need to piece borders for all four sides of the quilt. Press seams toward outside.

6. Mark the center edges of the borders and quilt top by folding them in half and inserting a pin at the fold.

7. With right sides together, match borders according to diagrams. Pin in place at beginning and end of seamline. Be sure to match center pins.

8. Baste and stitch two opposite borders in place, beginning and ending seams 1/4" from ends.

9. Press seams flat with seam allowances toward the borders.

10. Repeat with remaining two borders. (Seams will all begin and end at the ends of the two previously stitched border seams.) Anchor these points with a pin.

11. Working on one corner at a time, fold top border under to form a mitered corner.

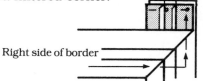

Right side of border

12. Align seamlines of border strips (see arrows). Pin as shown. Press fold, remove pins and press a firm crease at fold.

13. Leave pins in borders as shown in diagram.

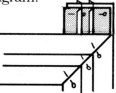

14. Fold borders with right sides together. Open seams and fold away from border. Insert pins through edges of border strips. Check underneath to see if pins are aligned with seams.

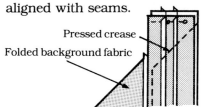

Pressed crease
Folded background fabric

15. Baste pressed crease. Stitch on basting, outward from design area to border edges. Remove basting. Trim 1/4" away from seam.

16. Press all seams in one direction; do not press them open.

17. Follow the directions given in the Glossary for Preparing to Quilt and Quilting.

18. Finish quilt with bias binding.

Checkerboard Wall Hanging

Finished size: 15 1/2" x 23 1/2"

Materials:
1/4 yd. red fabric
1/4 yd. green fabric
1/2 yd. fabric for trim and backing
3/8 yd. muslin for underlay
1/2 yd. needlepunch
12 1/2" x 12 1/2" fusible webbing
Optional: 15 1/2" wood dowel

Directions:
1. From both red and green fabric, cut eight strips, each 3" x 13".
2. Press to make doublefold strips following directions given in the Glossary.
3. Cut fusible webbing and muslin underlay, each 12 1/2" x 12 1/2".
4. Place fusible webbing on underlay. Place vertical rows of alternating red and green doublefold strips over the fusible webbing and secure one end of each strip with pins.
5. Weave horizontal rows of alternating red and green doublefold strips. Secure ends with pins.

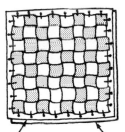

Fusible webbing   Muslin underlay

6. After checkerboard is woven, carefully remove pins and press to bond doublefold strips to fabric underlay. Trim any excess on strips even with underlay.
7. Cut needlepunch and backing 16" x 24". Center checkerboard on needlepunch and baste in place.
8. Cut two strips 2 1/2" x 12 1/2" and two strips 6" x 16" for trim.

9. With right sides together and using a 1/4" seam, sew the smaller strips to each side of checkerboard.
10. With right sides together and using a 1/4" seam, sew larger strips to each end of checkerboard.
11. Follow directions in Glossary to machine applique a heart to each end of checkerboard.
12. With right sides together, pin backing to checkerboard and stitch in a 1/4" seam, leaving an opening on one side for turning.
13. Clip corners. Turn to right side. Press.
14. Topstitch 1/4" from finished edges.
15. Checkerboard may be used as a wall hanging or table runner. If used as a wall hanging, hand stitch a 2" x 15 1/2" casing cut from backing fabric to back of checkerboard. Insert wood dowel.

Braided Heart Rug

Finished size: 36" x 26"

Materials:
Wool scraps in plaids; also
    burgundy, green, and biege*
Carpet thread
Carpet needle

Directions:
1. Wash woolens with warm water and regular laundry soap in your washing machine. Wash lights and darks separately.
2. Rip clean wool into strips: 1 1/2" to 1 3/4" wide if very heavy, 2" to 2 1/4" wide if medium weight.
3. Join strips of fabric (3 to 6 feet long), torn along straight grain, by machine-stitching on bias. Then fold strips as shown to make 1/2" strand with no raw edge.

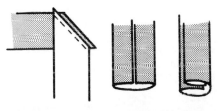

4. Roll strips of each fabric into a spiral for easier handling.
5. To start the braid, sew one folded strip at right angles to two other joined strips. Pin or clamp, then start braiding.

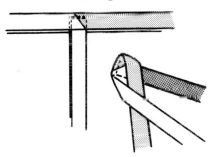

6. Braiding: with top of braid held firmly by pin or clamp, braid strips, keeping them even and straight. Secure each spiral with a safety pin so folds stay in place while you work.

7. The shape of the center dictates the final shape, so center section should be pinned in a wide V. Using a large needle and carpet thread, lace together adjoining braids. For smooth turns around the heart's curve, braid an extra turn on outside of curve for the first few rows. (See arrows.)

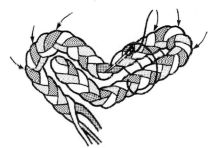

*Wool Strips for rugs can be cut from old woolen coats, jackets, blankets, pants, and dresses. Mill end stores are another thrifty source for wool fabrics.

Glossary of Techniques

Machine Applique

1. Several projects in this book are appliqued. To speed up the applique process, for control, and for accuracy, I recommend using a fusible webbing to adhere the cut pieces of applique fabric to the background fabric. Fusible webbing is available by the yard at most fabric stores. Follow the manufacturer's directions when using this product.

2. Always have an interfacing, fabric stabilizer, or tear-away product underneath the surface of your applique work. (I frequently use unbleached muslin.) This will prevent your stitches from bunching up in the back and puckering the background fabric. Trim away the excess around the edges of this backing stabilizer once all of the applique stitching is done.

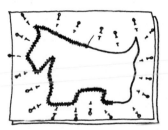

3. When machine applique stitching around the fabric, always use a tight zigzag stitch which forms a solid band of thread when sewn. (Test your stitch on a scrap of fabric first.) The width of your stitch should evenly cover the raw edges of your fabric.

4. When you begin your applique stitching, start with the areas that will lie underneath a dominant section of the pieced surface. Center the applique on your project, then lightly trace the outline of applique on fabric. This will serve as a guideline for your applique pieces. Always cover previously sewn seam ends and backstitch when you end each seam to avoid unraveling.

Paper Patch Applique

You may also applique by hand. I prefer using a technique called Paper Patch Applique.

1. Make templates for all pattern pieces from medium weight bond paper. Do not add seam allowance.

2. Place templates on fabric and draw 1/4" from all edges of template with an appropriate marking device.

3. Cut all fabric pieces along the drawn line.

4. Pin fabric to template

5. Fold 1/4" seam allowances over template. Baste fabric to template, using a running stitch and sewing through the paper.

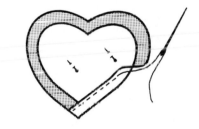

6. Clip inner curves and indentations, gently stretching fabric.

7. On outer curves, ease in fullness, using a small running stitch to gather the fabric. Do not sew through paper on outer curves. The basting stitches that go through the paper on either end of the outer curve will hold the fabric to the paper.

8. Baste all fabric pieces to paper. Do not use a knot after the last basting stitches since the basting stitches and paper must be removed in a later step.

9. Press all fabric pieces, easing fabric to ensure that bumpy edges are not created during pressing.

10. Applique fabric pieces to background, using a small blind stitch and matching thread. Stitches should be fairly close together. When applique of each piece is almost complete, pull basting thread from fabric and remove paper from the small opening that remains. A pair of tweezers is helpful for this step. If you completed the applique and forgot to remove the paper, make a small slit through the back side of the background fabric and remove paper with tweezers.

Yoyos

To make yoyos:

A. Using template, trace circle onto wrong side of fabric. Cut batting from corresponding template.

B. Pin batting to center of wrong side of each fabric circle.

C. Turn raw edges toward inside and secure with a small running stitch around the entire edge of the circle. Use a double thread for strength. Pull thread tightly to gather up the fabric and form a small hole in the center. Secure with several back stitches and a knot.

D. Evenly space the gathers around the center hole.

Clipping Techniques

Many sewn items in this book must have corners or curved seams clipped before being turned to the right side. Proper clipping will assure more accurate assembly and a smoother finish when the project is complete.

When clipping corners, remember that excess fabric left in a corner will cause bulk after the piece is turned.

For clipping curved seams, pinking shears will trim the seam and clip the curve in one easy step. In place of pinking shears, use scissors to trim excess fabric away from seams and clip the curves at 1/4" intervals.

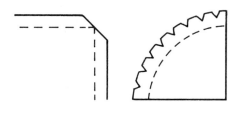

Trim Application

Many projects are enhanced by stitching trims and gathered laces into a seam.

1. Pin trim or lace to the right side of the project along the seamline. The finished edge of the lace or trim should be toward the inside.

2. Extra gathered lace or trim should be eased into corners. Ruffles and lace edges should be carefully pinned so they will not be caught in the stitching.

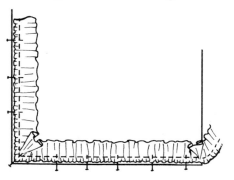

3. Take time to hide the beginning and end of the trim. Do not start and stop at the corners on square pieces; instead, overlap along a straight edge.

4. Baste trims or gathered laces in place.

5. With right sides together, pin backing or lining to front of project. Stitch in a 1/4" seam, leaving an opening for turning.

6. Turn project through opening. Trim or gathered lace will be sewn into the seam. If the edge of ruffle or trim has been caught in the seam, carefully open seam in this area. Reposition edge of trim and re-stitch.

Stuffing Techniques

Mountain Mist® Fiberloft® stuffing is recommended for projects in this book that require stuffing. The polyester fiberfill stuffing is light, fluffy and soft to the touch; it is available in 12-ounce or 16-ounce plastic bags at fabric stores.

When stuffing large or small areas, use small amounts of stuffing at a time. Use a narrow wooden dowel, wooden spoon handle or chopstick to position stuffing. Work the fiberfill into seams and blank areas while feeling for lumps on the outside of the fabric.

Bias Binding

Encasing raw edges in bias binding is an attractive and convenient way to finish many projects.

It's easy to make your own bias binding. Fold over a corner of fabric to find the true bias. Make a crease at the fold. Open the fold and cut along the crease. Measure 2"-wide strips and mark with a pencil. A transparent ruler and a rotary cutter are especially helpful for cutting bias strips.

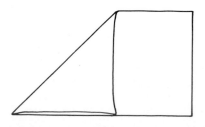

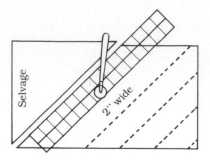

With right sides together machine stitch the bias strip ends in 1/4" seams. Press the seams open and trim away excess fabric. For projects in this book, make a folded bias binding by pressing a crease down the center of the strip with wrong sides together. When pressing, be careful not to stretch bias.

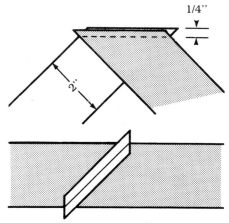

To finish edges with bias binding, sew the binding strips to the front of the project, placing right sides together and using a 1/4" seam. Be careful not to stretch the bias or the project edge as you sew. Overlap the binding at the corners.

Fold the bias binding over the raw edges of the project with the raw edge of the binding on the inside and the fold of the binding at the previous stitching line. Secure edge with a blind stitch, using thread that matches the binding, or with fusible webbing.

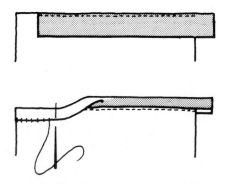

Double Fold Fabric Strips

These strips are not cut on the bias.

1. Press a crease down the center of a 2" fabric strip. Open fabric so that it is flat, wrong side facing up.

2. Fold raw edges over to the crease line. Press.

3. Crease in half along original crease line. Press. Stitch close to folded edges.

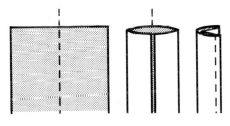

Crochet

Chain Stitch: Make a slip knot. Insert hook in long length of yarn and pull it through the loop.

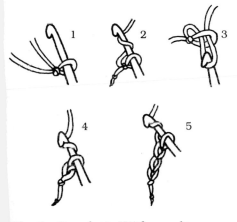

Single Crochet: With one loop on hook, insert hook into a stitch, hook long length of yarn and pull it through the stitch (you now have two loops on hook). Hook yarn again and pull it through both loops.

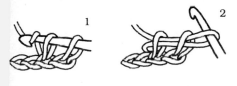

Slip Knot

Preparing to Quilt

Quilting can be done by hand or machine. The preparation for each is the same.

Press the quilt top. Lightly mark the quilting lines, using a blue water-erasable pen, a white marking pencil or a #2 lead pencil. Placement of the quilting lines will depend upon the quilt top design, the type of batting used and the amount of quilting desired.

Quilting supply stores carry stencils for quilting designs, including hearts, flowers and feathered wreaths, which are quite easy to use. You may prefer to mark the quilt top with an allover design such as a grid of squares or diamonds or parallel diagonal lines. No marking is necessary for quilting 1/4" away from each side of every seamline. Avoid quilting too close to the seamlines, where the bulk will slow you down.

Keep in mind that the purpose of quilting, besides its aesthetic value, is to securely hold the three layers of the quilt together. Do not leave large spaces unquilted.

Prepare the backing first. Plan to utilize a single length of 45"-wide fabric for the backing. Cut the backing 1" larger all the way around than the quilt top. Press thoroughly with the seams open. Lay the backing face down on a large, clean, flat surface. Tape the backing down with masking tape, being careful to keep it from stretching. It is important to keep the backing smooth and flat while working with other layers.

Cut the batting the same size as the backing and lay it on top. Smooth it out as well as you can.

Center the freshly ironed and marked quilt top face up on top of the batting. Beginning in the middle, pin baste the three layers together while gently smoothing the fullness to the sides and corners as you go. After pinning, baste the layers together with needle and light-colored thread. Begin in the center and make radiating lines of stitches. Remove the pins. Now you are ready to quilt.

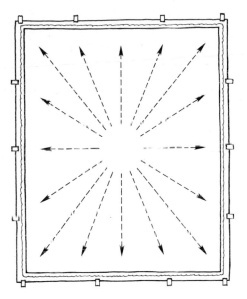

Quilting

Quilting is done with straight, even running stitches through all three quilt layers: quilt top, batting and backing. Use a single strand of quilting thread, a #8 quilting needle (between) and a thimble. Insert needle several inches from the point at which you wish to begin quilting. Pull the thread through the middle batting layer, bring needle out at starting point, take a backstitch and begin quilting.

To end quilting, insert needle into batting and pull thread through batting for several inches. Bring needle out through quilt top, insert needle in back side of point where thread came through quilt top and pull thread through batting several times. This makes the tiniest of backstitches, which are hardly visible on quilt top (see diagram).

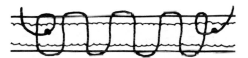

Polyester batting will hold thread. Clip thread close to quilt top. Whenever possible, begin and end quilting stitches in a seam. Quilting can be done in a hoop or on a frame.

Bows

Two yards of ribbon makes a nice full loopy bow. Pinch ribbon together between fingers approximately 2" from one end of ribbon. Continue to hold ribbon in one hand and make a loop in the ribbon with the other hand; pinch ribbon and hold securely. Add another loop to the other side of the bow and pinch as before. Twist ribbon as necessary to keep right side of ribbon to the outside of the bow.

Continue making loops, alternating from side to side and pinching each one firmly in the center, until at least five loops have been made on each side. An optional streamer may be added by centering a one-yard piece of ribbon behind the bow at this point.

To secure bow, wrap floral wire around pinched center of bow and twist wire firmly. Pull loops gently to form a pleasing arrangement.

Meet the Author

After studying home economics and textile design, Sue Saltkill's desire was to share her enjoyment of creative sewing with others. A designer, teacher, and author, Sue has written several successful books for That Patchwork Place, Inc.

Sue's first publication, **Log Cabin Constructions** was based on machine projects for the versatile Log Cabin block. Her second book, an outstanding bestseller, **Country Christmas** continued her work in the Log Cabin theme with projects adapted to the holiday season.

Sue Saltkill and co-author Nancy Martin recently produced her third publication, **Linens and Old Lace.** A delightful blend of the old and new, **Linens and Old Lace** combines contemporary designs with vintage "treasures from the trunk" in over 100 projects and ideas.

That Patchwork Place Publications

B50	**Sew Easy Strip Quilting** by Nancy Martin	$ 5.00
B54	**Barnyard Beauties** by Mary Ann Farmer	4.00
B56	**Fabriscapes™** by Gail Johnson	5.00
B57	**Be An Angel** by Mary Ann Farmer	4.00
B58	**Special Santas** by Mary Ann Farmer	4.00
B61	**Log Cabin Constructions** by Sue Saltkill	6.00
B62	**The Basics of Quilted Clothing** by Nancy Martin	8.00
B65	**Small Quilts** by Marsha McCloskey	6.00
B66	**Pilots, Partners & Pals** by Mary Ann Farmer	4.00
B68	**Warmest Witches to You** by Mary Ann Farmer	4.00
B69	**Fabric Frames From Stretcher Bars** by Susan A. Grosskopf	5.00
B70	**Country Christmas** by Sue Saltkill	6.00
B71	**Wall Quilts** by Marsha McCloskey	8.00
B72	**Cathedral Window - A New View** by Mary Ryder Kline	6.00
B73	**Signs of Our Times** by Susan A. Grosskopf	6.00
B74	**The Stencil Patch** by Nancy Martin	6.00
B75	**Sew Special** by Susan A. Grosskopf	6.00
B76	**A Quilter's Christmas** by Nancyann Twelker	8.00
B77	**Housing Projects** by Nancy J. Martin	9.95
B78	**Projects for Blocks and Borders** by Marsha McCloskey	11.95
B79	**Linens and Old Lace** by Nancy Martin and Sue Saltkill	9.95
B80	**A Touch of Fragrance** by Marine Bumbalough	5.95
B81	**Bearwear** by Nancy J. Martin	7.95
B83	**Christmas Quilts** by Marsha McCloskey	11.95

Printed in the United States of America